CONVERSATIONS BEFORE SILENCE

THE SELECTED POETRY
OF OLES ILCHENKO

CONVERSATIONS BEFORE SILENCE

THE SELECTED POETRY OF OLES ILCHENKO

CONVERSATIONS BEFORE SILENCE:
THE SELECTED POETRY OF OLES ILCHENKO

by Oles Ilchenko

Translated by Michael M. Naydan

Guest introduction by Kostyantyn Moskalets

Translations edited by Alla Perminova

Book cover and layout design by Max Mendor

© 2017, Michael M. Naydan

© 2017, Glagoslav Publications B.V.

www.glagoslav.com

ISBN: 978-1-911414-60-5

A catalogue record for this book is available from the British Library.

This book is in copyright. No part of this publication may be reproduced, stored in a retrieval system or transmitted in any form or by any means without the prior permission in writing of the publisher, nor be otherwise circulated in any form of binding or cover other than that in which it is published without a similar condition, including this condition, being imposed on the subsequent purchaser.

A BIOGRAPHICAL NOTE ON OLES ILCHENKO

Ukrainian poet, prose writer, children's author, culturologist, and filmscript writer Oles Ilchenko was born in Kyiv on October 4, 1957. He has lived in Kyiv for most of his life and traveled extensively to numerous other countries. He has spent the last several years living in Switzerland with his wife. He received degrees from the Drahomaniv Kyiv Pedagogical University and the Maxim Gorky Literary Institute in Moscow. He is the author of twenty-two children's books, the novels *City with Chimeras* (2009) and *My Beloved Kyara* (2011) and a book of memoirs of the 1970s-1990s, *Collectors of the Mists: Subjective Notes from a Life in Kyiv* (2017). His seven books of poetry include: *A Wintry Garden* (1991), *Constellation AS* (1993), *A Different Landscape* (1997), *Pages* (2004), *Cities and Islands* (2004), *Conversation before Silence* (2005), and *Certain Dreams, or A Kyiv which is Not* (2007). He also writes film scripts and is the author of numerous articles on cultural issues. His favorite pastimes include traveling to different countries, swimming, and experimenting with the creation of various culinary dishes.

ACKNOWLEDGEMENTS

My translations of "When the nurse pulls the needle from your vein" and "a. my grandfather died in 1969" appeared first in Zoland Poetry Annual. My translations of the poems "hauling bodies through landscapes," "I took down my portrait," and "to find" appeared first in the journal of translation Metamorphoses, and my translations of the poems "slowly…," "it's worth it…," CAIRO, "but then to separate…," and "in making love with you…" were first published in International Poetry Review. Many thanks to Kost Moskalets for allowing me to translate and publish his fine piece on Ilchenko's poetry. Much gratitude to Svitlana Budzhak-Jones and Alla Perminova for their extremely helpful comments on the translation of the introduction. Extra special thanks to Alla Perminova for her perspicacious suggestions for emendations to my translations of the poetry, which serve to make them much better. I, of course, am responsible for any errors that may have slipped through the cracks.

CONTENTS

A BIOGRAPHICAL NOTE ON OLES ILCHENKO 5

ACKNOWLEDGEMENTS 6

THE POETRY OF OLES ILCHENKO:
SOME OBSERVATIONS ON A POET-TRAVELER 10

EXPERIENCING THE RAPTUROUS NOW 13

FROM THE COLLECTION *PAGES* **(2004)** 21
    "YOU ASK WHY" 22
    "IN MY FAVORITE CAFÉ" 23
    "TO THE BARKING DOGS AT NIGHT" 24
    "WHEN I LOOK AT A MOTH AT NIGHT" 25
    "AT NIGHT YOU SHOULD WANDER" 26
    "A SHADOW" 27
    "THERE WAS A PRE-HISTORIC TIME WHEN" 28
    "THE MOUTH OF A DROWNED PERSON" 29

FROM THE COLLECTION *CITIES AND ISLANDS* **(2004)** 31
    NIGHT STATION 32
        "WHEN THE NURSE PULLS THE NEEDLE FROM YOUR VEIN" . . 32
        "ONE FEBRUARY MORNING I DIED AND" 33
        "THREE DRUNKARDS BAREFOOT" 34
        "THEY LAID YOU TO REST. IT RAINED THAT DAY" 35
        "WHEN YOU DIED, I STARTED TO WRITE" 36
    PASSAGE 37
        "SLOWLY" 37
        "THE LAST CROSSING" 38

"A. MY GRANDFATHER DIED IN 1969" 39

"AFTER ALL WE ARE BORN IN THE CITY" 40

"IT'S WORTH IT" 40

CITIES AND ISLANDS 43

   SEVEN CAPITALS 44

      AMSTERDAM 44

      BERLIN 45

      BRUSSELS 47

      CAIRO 48

      LUXEMBOURG 49

      MADRID 50

      PARIS 52

   SEVEN ISLANDS 53

      GRAN CANARIA 53

      TENERIFE 54

      LANZAROTE 55

      LA GOMERA 56

      LA PALMA 57

      EL HIERO 59

      FUERTEVENTURA 61

FROM THE COLLECTION *CONVERSATION*
BEFORE SILENCE **(2005)** 63

   I. A GREEN BOAT 64

      "HAULING BODIES THROUGH LANDSCAPES" 64

      "I TOOK DOWN MY PORTRAIT" 65

      "TO FIND" 66

      "BUT THEN TO SEPARATE" 67

      "BENEATH SOFT VELVET WINGS" 68

      "AT FIRST FOXTAIL AND BLUEGRASS" 69

    "WITH THE KEY OF MEMORY OPENING" 70

    "IN THE OLIVE-COLORED WATER" 71

II. TIME IN RIME 72

    "SHE'S SLEEPING CLOSE BY" 72

    "TO ENTER INTO THE WARM ALLURING SEA" 73

    "WHEN I MAKE LOVE WITH YOU" 74

    "IT'S REALLY SWEET" 75

    "WE TURN OUT THE LIGHT" 76

    "WE'RE DRINKING ZAKARPATSKY COGNAC" 77

FROM THE COLLECTION *CERTAIN DREAMS,*
OR A KYIV WHICH IS NOT **(2007)** 79

    "THEY'RE BURNING FALLEN LEAVES IN THE GARDEN" 80

    "TO POUR OUT SOME BLOOD—TO DRINK WINE." 81

    "THOSE CROWS THAT LIVE ON REITARSKA STREET" 82

    "IN THE DEAD CAFÉ" 83

    "POURED TEA, COLD COFFEE" 84

    "GULP, DRINK UP. DON'T MENTION ANYONE" 85

FROM POEMS NOT PUBLISHED IN COLLECTIONS 87

    "YOU SLEEP CAPRICIOUSLY" 88

    "SEDGE" 89

    "AN OVERLY SHARP SENSE OF LIFE" 90

    "THOSE COLORS ARE GRAY" 91

    "THE TASTE OF ACHING IN THE MIDDLE OF" 93

THE POETRY OF OLES ILCHENKO:
SOME OBSERVATIONS ON A POET-TRAVELER

I once asked my good friend the poet Viktor Neborak to suggest some interesting newer poets emerging on the literary scene in Ukraine. Viktor, without even taking time to think about it, uttered the name of just one poet to me—Oles Ilchenko from Kyiv. Trusting Viktor's judgment and his refined literary taste, I jotted down the name in a notepad and went to a bookstore the next day where I found copies of the poet's books. After perusing and buying them, I dove into them and immediately was impressed by Ilchenko's poetry, which was profoundly philosophical and personal, as well as spare and direct in terms of its imagery and metaphors. The poet's voice was assured and steady, and it spoke directly to the reader much in the way that Lina Kostenko's and Anna Akhmatova's poetry did. The biggest surprise to me was a Ukrainian poet writing in the natural rhythms of the language without traditional rhyme and meter, the latter of which dominated Ukrainian poetry until the most recent transitional and current younger generation of poets. Ilchenko himself notes some of the possible influences on him in his shift to free verse through his own allusions to William Carlos Williams and Stanley Kunitz in his poems. One would be hard pressed to imagine two better poet "mentors" from the American tradition to aid in the poet's transition to new poetic forms.

Ilchenko is one of the best Ukrainian poets writing in free verse today. His poetry is associative, flitting, and fragmentary. At times he does not form complete sentences in his poems and links words together into phrases before shifting into another thought or idea. The language of his poetry has a tendency to collapse into itself, often forcing the reader to reevaluate a word or line, to reread a previous word or phrase to focus on the poet's inner logic. This fragmentary incompleteness and permeability mimics much the way human consciousness works without the filter of the written communicative convention of sentences and grammatical structure. This "slipperiness" and rapid shifting of voice comprises one of the essential invariants in Ilchenko's poetics. The poet also flaunts many traditional poetic Ukrainian conventions. Like ee cummings he tends to avoid capital letters or punctuation such as exclamation points. One will find only commas and dashes for pauses, and an occasional period in his poems, which do not always end with the finality of that punctuation mark. In doing this, the poet often suggests a fragment or slice of his life broken off on the page and to be continued at some point in time.

The imagery of Ilchenko's poetry, too, is devoid of excessive embellishments and rhetorical flourishes. He presents to his reader precisely what he is feeling or perceiving at a given moment, whether that be his own unfiltered pain and psychological state in a hospital emergency room or his elation at discovering the essence of places he visits in his native Kyiv, the capitals of Europe, or the Canary Islands. He fuses the visual with the aural in his poetry and conveys scenes with a roving consciousness that describes and subtly interprets. One always senses the poet's physical presence, his eyes, in the vivid scene he describes, as if he were a camera filming it. Perhaps his background in writing film scripts and the film industry gives him that pictorial focus on the slices of the interpreted world that he presents in his poetry. While certain of his poems are elegiac or confessional, they do not lead him to the depths of darker mental states, but rather serve as points of departure for a continuation of his life's journey and an expiation of that deeply felt emotion left behind on paper or in the computer and later on the printed page. The experience of the death of loved ones and one's own infirmity clearly spurs the poet's writing process, particularly in the first part of the collection *Cities and Islands* (2004). Consciousness of his own mortality leads him to understand that the meaning of life can only be found in living one's own life. He discovers that human beings must continue on with their lives after emotional pauses as well as profound losses. The only answer to death can only be life and in living the latter with passion and love. To that end the reader, particularly in the poet's later poems, finds the omnipresence of a beloved other, whom he is found observing. Readers will find sexuality and eroticism in Ilchenko's works, but a much more restrained male eroticism than other postmodern Ukrainian writers who focus on the pure physicality of sex and not the emotionality. That attraction, that psychological bond with his love, marks the fulfillment of being that is a powerful means of overcoming loneliness in the vast cosmos, one's own personal method of not raging, but coping with the dying of the light of those close to him. There is decanting in several of Ilchenko's poems—the pouring and drinking of vodka, wine, cognac, and coffee in cafes along with degustation—these all comprise a part of both necessary nourishment as well as the celebration of life. The poet, too, often is a traveler, whose peregrinations give him new life experience and physically take him away from the locus of his former emotional losses and pain. Those travels also serve to spark the creative imagination, the results of which comprise a significant part of this collection of selected poetry. Ilchenko is a fascinating poet whose idiom and unique manner of expression in Ukrainian translates seamlessly into the poetics of contemporary English.

– Michael M. Naydan
Woskob Family Professor of Ukrainian Studies
The Pennsylvania State University

EXPERIENCING THE RAPTUROUS NOW

The new collection of poems by Kyivan poet Oles Ilchenko *Cities and Islands* comprises his fifth book of poetry. Before that he published *Winter Garden* (1991), *Constellation AS*[1] (1993), *A Different Landscape* (1997) and, after seven years of silence, a book of photographs and poems *Pages* (2004). *Pages* appeared shortly before *Cities and Islands* and immediately attracted the attention of poetry aficionados as a result of the author's quite original design, lyric poems interspersed with rare photographs of Kyivan architectural monuments that disappeared from the urban landscape in recent decades and that were unable to withstand the savage attack of our rabidly capitalistic civilization. The dominant nostalgic aching inherent in *Pages* was caused by the irreversible nature of the disappearance of landscapes of childhood and youth; we recognize it on the first pages of *Cities and Islands*. But this time, the nostalgic aching engendered much more dramatic cataclysms, those generated from places of the heart, not just from buildings that no longer exist. This first part of the book is about the death of people closest to us, about this unbearable but unavoidable primer of human existence that each of us must learn over the course of our lives, knowing in advance that the last letter will be "я" (I; the last letter of the Ukrainian alphabet) even when you apply the magic of the mirror of grammatology or when you try symbolically to replace the letters of the Cyrillic with those of the Latin alphabet as in the following poem:

    a. my grandfather died in 1969
    b. my mother's father lived 84 years
    c. one grandmother suffered away
    d. the other was terribly ill before that
    e. my mother's gone after she took ill
    f. and my father would be alive if
    g. it's clear whose turn it is now

---

[1] The constellation "AS" is mentioned in Job 9:9 in Slavic bibles and rendered in most English bibles as the Bear or Great Bear.

h. all the same it's strange to step to the front of the line
i. when someone asks me who's last
j. I answer in a whisper
k. it's insulting not to die but to forget everything
l. maybe memory anyway is kept there
m. what feeling do I take with me
n. to the heavenly city
o. to the islands of hell

Memory does not just gather the dead at the table ("I sit in a circle of the dead..."); it brings together the living world of man, a mysterious one not subject to analysis, in this way creating entire hearts from disparate (according to point of view) feelings, thoughts and events. Memory consists of the Word uttered in a single breath, and therefore, it is a blissful amnesia, the keenly needed oblivion of the laws of death's morphology. Therefore, for the poet the question of preserving the gift of personal, unblemished memory *there*—"beyond the heavens, beyond the stars" is vitally urgent. However, to preserve memory means to be made whole yourself and simultaneously to save your beloved dead. Therefore it is a bit awkward to interpret Ilchenko's book, in particular the first part subtitled "Night Station," as a collection of essentially artistic works. That section is a miniature book within a book, reminding us of a prayer book of a contemporary secular man; a prayer, according to the accurate observation of Bakhtin refers to actions rather than artistic works. In "Night Station" the phenomenology of that, which dies is alienated; sometimes even the ironic description of an unengaged observer is replaced by the involvement of a person who utters prayers for the dead. Those prayers as a real application of memory and word emerge beyond the latent state of alienation, exploding in a burst of ecstasy for him who no longer is ("How oddly he's mentioned there..."). Noting the presence of the infrastructure of death that wraps around the living world and occasionally becomes visible, Ilchenko consciously highlights the most unessential of its signs ("After standing in the cemetery everyone greedily gulped down hot cabbage soup") so as to suddenly find what is left in the shade as impossibly unreal—identification with the dead person:

> One February morning I died and
> stared at myself for a long time, at

> the sharpened features of an indifferent face.
> I didn't shudder in fright when I touched myself, though
> Itried hard to remember something, but
> couldn't; I wanted to say something, but
> felt it to be inappropriate.
> Inaccessible for those in my past expired here
> irony fills the hereafter.
> Really enjoyable was the absolute
> light, much higher than rays in
> the windows of intensive care on the top floor...

Oles Ilchenko belongs to a series of poets whose talent continues to mature from collection to collection, passing stages of growth unhurriedly and least of all not focusing on whimsical poses and the demands of quickly changing literary fashions. These poets never appear instantaneously ready, fully equipped for versification. Cherishing their constant unpreparedness of being, they therefore remain receptive longer to changes and renewal; they gradually acquire new techniques, systems of rhyme, and metrical forms so that, having mastered them totally and having provided the most perfected example of a given form, immediately and for a long time ignore their laboriously obtained know-how to return to different themes, to a fundamentally different instrumentation. *Cities and Islands* is a book entirely written in free verse, while Ilchenko's previous collections were written in more traditional forms. His poetry of the 1990s is reminiscent of the fresh, vigorous sprout of the neoclassical tree. It patterned itself on the loftiest achievements of the Silver Age of Russian literature (particularly on the masterpieces of Anna Akhmatova) and the Golden Age of Ukrainian literature (here we should first mention the undeniable influence of Maxym Rylsky and Lina Kostenko). However, the transition to free verse is not the only innovation that catches your eye. In *Cities and Islands* the poet repeatedly returns to his earlier works, rewriting them in a new key, "translating," adorning them in richer semitones and penumbra, occasionally radically changing the original version. For example, you can compare these two poems, the first of which was published in the collection *Constellation AS*:

> there's snow in the yard
> and three kings with gifts

walk along the empty street
passing the only house with lights
in the city
it's cold now
as if summer had never been
we are left only to follow the kings
with our eyes
the last night will judge everyone
and for the wormwood of the looking glass
will give everyone
Ukraine
for the infant in her arms already is evil

A modified version of the same text in *Cities and Islands* sounds fundamentally different:

Three barefoot drunkards…
Where are they going and why?
They're teased and called "kings." They
avoid all the buildings with lights,
skulk next to certain gray walls
of the city at night.
They place a candle at every ruin.
They try to plead their case—for an evil infant.
Maybe they're right.
Who is able to understand them?

As you can see, the initially elevated image, made in the spirit of a modernized Christmas crèche scene is markedly "brought down" in the second version. The Kings from the East appear as grotesquely ordinary drunkards who comprised "three" and are only nicknamed "kings." However, the surreal development of the scene (barefoot bums place candles at every ruin for the "evil infant"—the Antichrist given birth by Ukraine in the previous version of the poem) informs the grotesque with a tragic and menacing sound, no less expressive than the original elegiac version. In subsequent editions such "paired" verses should be printed next to each other in order to maintain the obvious nature of the dialectic and synthesis of productive, creative efforts and to emphasize the continuity of their own tradition, read now only by isolated experts of Ilchenko's works.

Despite the rather gloomy thanatology of the first part of *Cities and Islands*, it especially makes the strongest impression, not in the least due to the particular density and laconic nature of poetic expression. An almost complete lack of metaphors, sparse and precise comparisons, a weary aphoristic nature, and a uniquely "novelistic" quality—all these and many other features of Ilchenko's new writing create a surprisingly capacious image of a structured work, which, according to Les Herasymchuk, "grows from late conceptualism and is close to virtual poetry that is slowly replacing postmodernism." However, in the new collection there is no shortage of specific signs of postmodernism, which are profusely scattered in the two following sections "Passage" and "Cities and Islands." This can be the bewitching sound patterning that resembles the magical effect of serial music as well as many eloquent allusions and hidden quotations—as in Kyivan urban folklore, or with sculptural groupings in Madrid—or an intertextual game with poems by William Carlos Williams or Wallace Stevens (most visibly manifested in the poem "How strangely he is mentioned there..."), semi-hints, semi-allusions to Nabokov, Domontovych, Gogol, flashes of youth slang or provocative puns and oxymorons ("Subsequently I began to feel something...," "glamour rustling rapidity...", "why don't you try to paint that way..."). I must admit, after the icy elevated nature of "Night Stations," the transition to colorful descriptions of exotic cities and islands (the cycle "Seven Capitals" and "Seven Islands"), to a nomadic carefree tourist, a gourmet, a lover of life, to the candidness of an expert on countless species of plants, animals and wine is perceived first as unintentional blasphemy or the inadequately planned structure of the book. It was only later, after prolonged thinking and rereading, despite the fact that directly in the text you begin to be inclined toward agreeing with the author's intention: it simply could not have been structured differently. After all, for our secular contemporary belief in the Islands of the Blessed, to where after death a righteous soul departs, is just a beautiful myth, one of many tokens of the ancient past. This belief can call on—like the Egyptian pyramids, "*gray triangles on a colorless sky.*" That is why one should seek and find those islands in life, here and now, so that on some La Palma, surrounded by the ocean, one can remember or surmise, confirm and verify with one's own personal experience something that the ancient Orphics, the Indian Brahmins and Egyptian high priests called:

> looking at the perfection
> of the waves and the sky
> of the round island amid the ocean
> the local climate
> and strong drinks
> you begin to guess
> in what the perfection
> of a person should lie
> here and
> somewhere ("La Palma")

The key word in this verse "perfection" is linked to spatial relationships, but it also suggests time coordinates, just imprecisely as a certain final "somewhere." "Somewhere" anticipates "everywhere and always." The experience of a good decentered nature, balance, and presence in being is reproduced by "La Palma," the experience of which is reminiscent of the lesson of mystics of all times, with one substantial caveat: the ecstatic unity with itself and the world is achieved today and is not postponed to the otherworld tomorrow. "He, who thirsts for 'a bigger life,' 'a more intensive life,' 'a higher life,' 'or a real life,' sees before himself... a number of non-religious forms of revitalization, which occupy a certain positive legacy of religion: this is art, science, the erotic, travels, corporeal culture, politics, psychotherapy, etc. They all can make their contribution to the reconstruction of that "fullness of life" that in religion was the focus of dreams and memory... A new study of life occurs through the great work of remembering, however, one that not only raises the sludge of the past. "The innermost recollection leads not to a story but to a force. To touch this force means to experience a flood of ecstasy. This experience ends up not in a past but in a rapturous now,"[2] Peter Sloterdijk has written in *Critique of Cynical Reason* by analyzing these phenomena over which readers of Ilchenko's poems reflect today.

Is it precisely the "rapturous now" that becomes the main persona in the final chapter of *Cities and Islands* that is realized in the generous flood of the resurrected? the commemorated? feelings seized in

---

2   I've opted to quote here from the English translation of Peter Sloterdijk's *Critique of Cynical Reason*. Michael Eldred trans. Minneapolis-London: U of Minnesota P, 1987: 287.

contemplation-relishing of a kaleidoscopically variegated and in its own way harmonious world. These poems breathe the openness of ocean spaces and immense capitals without losing the characteristic home warmth of realized cherished dreams. The life that flickers in this poetry is unaware of its finite nature—nor does it give it particular significance: "You are left to ascend to death at the final night station." ("It's desirable to celebrate your day of death...").

Life is not the antithesis of death; this line of thought would be too banal and is therefore false. Life comprises death in itself, it grows it like a tiny island amid the never before seen beauty of the ocean—and only thanks to this firmament underfoot does it make sense, in other words, have value. *Cities and Islands* by Oles Ilchenko without excess fuss professes belief in the value of every existence, every memory, every joy, and every death—everywhere and for always. Therefore, you should closely listen to this book—because such belief and similar experience are inherent among us all, and there are myriad opportunities for daily trials.

—Kostyantyn Moskalets,
from his book *The Game Continues:
Literary Criticism and Essays*. Kyiv: Fakt, 2006.

—Translated by Michael M. Naydan

FROM
THE COLLECTION *PAGES*
(2004)

***

you ask why
but why do they gather stones
on the seashore
either tiny shells or bits of coral
why do they look at the moon
or touch a grape leaf
maybe to remember
a memory-stone
a memory-seashell
a memory-branch that sinks
into the silver of the night sun
hieroglyphs of leafy veins know of
a wooden table under an olive tree
grayed from age
a bottle of chianti
a forgotten villager's cap on a chair
if you rid yourself of objects-memories
then what's the sense of anything
you'll say and what about the sound of waves
the scent of magnolias
resinous Italian pines
the saltiness of kisses after
swimming in the sea
yes indeed
but sound lives in the seashell
the eternity of our kisses
in the firmness and roundness of the shore's stones
and the scent of flowers and trees
in your
evening gaze

***

in my favorite café
that has a slight woman's touch
you have to walk a bit out of your way from zeil street[3]
you told me
strange stories from your life
I listened to them and didn't
I believed them and didn't
it doesn't happen that way
and who knows how a romance begins
with a woman
or a *roman*—a novel in your home computer
a romance as a genre of life
maybe it would be enough to say
paris and a writer writes
he loves just this kind of emigrant woman
in fact not any romances
just the muddy main river
swans on the water
coffee with cream
we just dropped in
to sit out the rain

---

[3] The most famous shopping street in Frankfurt am Main in Germany.

***

for Les Herasymchuk

to the barking of dogs of night
under the cynical gaze of the moon
black lines about yearning for a letter
stigmata appear on every page
every word is perfect
that's why it's hard to read the truth
and that's why there's nowhere to hide

a lamp shining in the face
hands tied behind the back of a chair
it didn't happen to me but to us
to the KGB you said
he just writes silly
poems about nature where he grew up

when it's cold the cricket grows silent
and the city's silent at four a.m.
even the echo of a shofar grows distant
to the invisible years ahead

***

For Kost Moskalets

When I look at a moth at night —
there it is, blinded,
sitting under the ceiling—
for some reason I think:
it was born scaly-winged in the branches
of the oak
at which that poet from Worcester, Mass[4]
aimed tiny stones.
The beautiful moth flew circles around a light bulb,
grew tired and dozed off.
Maybe it's dreaming of
its homeland of green leaves and
the scent of warm bark.
But you won't sit long;
you want to look
from under the clouds at
the poet standing
about a dozen steps from
the trunk with gravelly stones in his pocket.
Look, and walk aimlessly,
to other forests
to the deceptive light of settlements,
to elegant abodes, in which,
unfortunately, you can't find
either a green branch
or poets.

---

4   The poet has in mind American poet-laureate Stanley Kunitz and his poem "The Testing Tree." See: https://www.poets.org/poetsorg/poem/testing-tree for a copy of the poem online.

***

at night you should wander
through rooms
and randomly turn toward your books
take several off the shelves
suddenly you find one unread
you feverishly flip
the white flour
pages
dotted with black poppy grains
of opium thoughts
you calm the shudder
having come across
the authentic
with green tea you wash
insomnia from your eyes
you feel the book covers
swallow pills
and let into your chest
the sweet horror of real poems

***

a shadow
on the ground
on the asphalt
on someone's face
maybe the remains of a stone wall
the museum of a wall
the history of a past illness
corrected grammar
vanished punctuation marks
watersheds moved to the east
and into the chrome brandenburg gate
and the ishtar gate
in the pergamon museum
spring branches extended
at the crossroads of the next in turn
U-bahn and S-bahn
suddenly the melody of a hopak dance tune
and the musician is so dark-skinned that you
suddenly understand
the witty thought of a local drunk
across from you
who drinks beer in the morning
but the green sprouts branch out
distracting thoughts
you feel like simply
tearing a leaf
crumpling it
breathing in its aromas

***

there was a pre-historic time when
we climbed up castle hill
fell in the grass
gazed at the cupola-dome azure sky
and didn't even talk
so as not to frighten away
the happy moment
that came for no special
reason
it called on us for a minute
it was eternal summer
I felt like smiling
and I didn't even think that I'd call
you in London and congratulate you
for what I should have
that I'd promise to come
right away
but now
when even if
I climb up
crooked
weed-covered
castle-kiselivka hill[5]
there I wouldn't find
the sky
or a smile
or the gentle breeze of happiness

---

5 A hilly area in Kyiv overlooking the Dnipro River that has been known over time as Zamkova hora (castle hill), Kiselivka (a place where kissel is made), and Florivska hora (named after a nearby monastery). Many thanks to the poet for enlightening me on the various historical names.

***

the mouth of a drowned man
rises up out the water
utters sounds
of a dead language
letters like ashes
fly in the air
they settle on the water
black swollen slippery already
they are carried by a wave
to the shore
and an old woman
from a riverside tea shop
still recollects
an unbelievable august
yellow
just like her face

FROM
THE COLLECTION *CITIES AND ISLANDS*
(2004)

NIGHT STATION

***

When the nurse pulls the needle from your vein
a strange sensation occurs – pain,
then conversely, antipain, a faint
release. Though it doesn't last
very long.
Some kind of shadows flow
through lustrous hallways
of the hospital, and blend in thoughts
with similar specters from the building across the street.
On the ninth floor
at the end of the hallway
above a pitiful palm tree, an exile from its southern
homeland, there hangs a cheap print of Van Bock's
landscape "Empty December."
Something is wilting on the lush land,
but the branches of an old poplar
prevent you from looking through
the foreground or
to see anything warm-toned.
Maybe it's a Palm Sunday night's burning candle
that you have to carry
home.

***

One February morning I died and
stared at myself for a long time, at
the sharpened features of an indifferent face.
I didn't shudder in fright when I touched myself, though
I tried hard to remember something, but
couldn't; I wanted to say something, but
felt it to be inappropriate.
Irony inaccessible to those I left behind here
fills the hereafter.
Really enjoyable was the absolute
light, much higher than rays in
the windows of intensive care on the top floor.

***

Three drunkards barefoot...
Where are they going and why?
They're teased and called "kings." They
avoid all the buildings with lights,
lean toward certain gray walls
of the city at night.
They place a candle at every ruin.
They try to plead their case — for an evil infant.
Maybe they are right.
Who is able to understand them?

***

They laid you to rest. It rained that day;
people said that recollections fall
in an abundant rain. I remembered
the warmth of your body, your voice,
the way you used to shape the sound of words for me.
Now they also fell right
before me. I think
that nothing fades away other than bodies – not inside us,
not between us.
Ivy clings tightly to
a tree trunk and soars to the sky. The tree
eventually falls and pulls the winding branches
down behind it.
It remains for us only to wait,
just a little bit more.

***

After you died I started to write
you letters. About the illusory nature
of evening peace, the hailing
of nighttime commuter trains, about boredom
in a certain village on the Latoritsa River,
the borderline early morning hour
in the mountains, new borders.
About a cluster of strangely regular
car accidents—either the brakes
give out, or a tree simply crawls out
onto the road; they tell the truth:
when I die, at least bury me.[6]
Everything is old and eternal like funeral repasts,
banal, like drunken funeral mourners.
But for you how can I express a longing
not worthy of all these meaningless words?

---

6   A close paraphrase of the first line of Ukrainian national bard Taras Shevchenko's famous poem "My Testament," which begins: "After I die, bury me...."

PASSAGE

***

slowly
as the body goes deeper
into itself
and the spirit directs its flight
higher
and higher
the gaze changes
its field of vision rises up
and grows
the eyes of the soul
always keep watch from above
in contrast to childhood
when your sight is directed
from the earth to the clouds
and in time flies like an equal
to an equal

you want not to miss out out of mercy
a movement
or a second
of the absolute elevated nature of your new I

***

the last crossing
black
like that hole

faster
faster
a hastened not even movement
but flight
from the final city
to that last
and only island
firm among the waves
droplets in space

I've grasped by reason but
the heart shudders
be quiet
be quiet
you're just a heart

a whistling
movement
through

***

a. my grandfather died in 1969
b. my mother's father lived 84 years
c. one grandmother suffered away
d. the other was terribly ill before that
e. my mother's gone after she took ill
f. and my father would be alive if
g. it's clear whose turn it is now
h. all the same it's strange to step to the front of the line
i. when someone asks me who's last
j. I answer in a whisper
k. it's insulting not to die but to forget everything
l. maybe memory anyway is kept there
m. what feeling do I take with me
n. to the heavenly city
o. to the islands of hell

***

after all we are born in the same city
and travel through just that city
sometimes it takes the form
of a suburban forest
or the island of zeus between africa and europe

if you're lucky you can find
a worm passageway
an actual wormhole and
go back in time
to fix
something
change it
make amends
you can of course also
overtake yourself
and then pass by yourself
end up in the wrong
country
in the wrong faith
in the wrong time
be sad your entire life
listen to new CDs
watch new DVDs
write poems
asking yourself from time to time
like William Carlos Williams did
who do I write today

***

it's worth it
to wait
for a truly warm summer
evening
to step out to listen to the crickets
to find a handful of fresh clover
among the wheat grass and dandelions
to bury your face in
a trefoiled leaf
to sense its bittersweet
fragrance
taste
color
this is a true moment
such an authentic deep one
the opposite of so called life
that rushes like
a drop of quicksilver in
a matchbox
moving all around in its square circle

the clover leaf is eternal
because it's fresh
and the evenings warm
because they are ours

it is in just such a time I
desire
crave
want you
sensing the truth
of the two
of us

CITIES AND ISLANDS

SEVEN CAPITALS

AMSTERDAM

the souls of broken bicycles
languish at the bottom of the canals
gaze through periscopes of imagination
at multistory
parking decks of living brother-bicycles
what is even better
water circling all around
the iron frame-soul
an incessant ramayana
of the elements in motion
all around a freed essence or
illusory motion through the streets
from which one can go
to another dimension
only by
breaking off a chain
kicking off wheels
and then
joining the eternal
driving wheel
of streaming water

BERLIN

one more circle and
the bus returns to
the brandenburg gate
since the new year a friend has been living here
like you
for a hundred years and a day
a clumsy radiola box
in the museum of the wall
not for music
but for transporting a person through
how you got settled
a pretext to come to the berlinale
to watch films
now the city is just festivaling
just the movies
a museum island with
the gates of ishtar there somewhere
recreated in halls
prostitutes along the evening road
lining up peering into taxis
to get off at the magdalenenplatz station
to drink gross bier ja
to be astounded by
the eternal erection of the tv tower
by the beautiful zoo
by the smartly remodeled reichstag
by a melody of a hopak in the subway
new immigrant ethiopians
new jewish citizens

a capital restored
only a certain shadow
on the grass on the asphalt
that's really something
there's no old town
and a secret revealed
there
never was
a wall

BRUSSELS

a palace in which the king lives
a palace in which the king works
a palace in which the king is
simply a palace
it simply seems to be an efficient
imitation of paris
simply evening and some
pickpockets
a simple boy from waterloo
that's not far from here
will help change the tire of my car
simply a light quenching of thirst
with a stella
simply all too unpredictable weather
good music in the rain
a noble museum
an incomprehensible aching
a mini-europe park
about a dozen countries missing
maybe I'm missing or I'm missing something
I'm here and elsewhere simultaneously
in distant india
without even an attached
west- to it
a solid ost
that goes by east
and on the flipside of a paper euro for some reason
a bridge

CAIRO

the chaos
of senseless
ceaseless
aimless
streams of cars
no traffic cops
no road signs
no blinking traffic lights
the carousel of a scorching day
the swing of an uncertain chilling of the night
and the pink freshness of hibiscus tea
you can haggle
you can work out a discount
you can get something and forget
you can cross the nile
you can look at piles of trash
on the picturesque banks
a horse that sluggishly floats
belly up
warms itself in the sun
follows the flow
and then you should see mountains
on the horizon that
pretend to be a mirage
beyond the palm trees
gray triangles on a colorless sky
to remember the word
giza
again to notice the buzz
of the signs of the day
that in the end are reduced to
the pyramidic thingification
of eternity

LUXEMBOURG

The cone of a mountain or
a cylinder of hard cheese
just holes caves passages
nooks
crannies
alleyways
the worm of time ate away
land flesh maybe
it just wanted
to turn space inside out
a river
stone buildings
a palace
a shabby shy sentry
guarding the calm of the duke
a fairytale land
we'll cross it by car
in an hour or two
we'll cross it and what's beyond that
everywhere past the threshold it's different
but not dissimilar
even the sky is similar clouds
cloned
a conventional country
a conventional state
a conventional language
an unexpressed prayer
lord where do we hide
everything is so small
as big as an hour
why can't you see children here
probably just
jewelers candy makers tourists live here
and, of course one who eats time

MADRID

calm down run out
early in the morning from the hotel ritz
long look at the prado
then nibble on some churros or
roasted chestnuts
we'll stumble against the comic impossibility
to come to an understanding sometimes
that is neither fish nor fowl
the ringing like bronze[7] latin aptly becomes useful
for a mollusk
si molusko si sepia[8]
o cuttlefish si
o the semi-transparent jamon[9]
really melts in your mouth
a din in the coffee house
nearly identical to the shouts
on the morning square
before the appearance of the bound black-haired knight
the demon's cloven hooves noticed in time
the handsome man beneath the armor
confessing when he was placed in boots
the din of the tavern
waiters in a hurry
serving blood in wine glasses
they carry twigs to the purifying fire
and perhaps the cobblestones in front of the entrance
is extant from those times
here stand the stone lope[10] and christopher
pondering escape

---

7   An epithet used to describe Latin as a kind of perfect language that rings as purely as bronze. In the original the poet is imitating the ancient Greek hexameter. Thanks to the poet for explaining this to me.

8   Cuttlefish in Spanish.

9   Ham in Spanish.

10 The Spanish playwright Lope de Vega and Christopher Columbus.

or whether they'll be helped by
a gangly man with a spear
and a stout man on a donkey
however they are all phantoms
like the district of salamanca
like the fountains and parks with lakes
only real platan trees lean toward the sky
under eternal cathedrals
every night in silence
scream with the horrors of Goya
remembering something

PARIS

You can sit on your favorite
wooden bridge over the Seine
and just look
enough of a whole lot of word-symbols
signs-places
building-associations
enough of meetings
unless this one is
over onion soup in a cupola
just look at
the cranks
musicians
lovers
grandmothers
second-hand booksellers
you should lie on the warm planks of the bridge
and daydream about nothing
shouldn't I go in the evening
to the restaurant on the corner of
saint-germain and saint-michel
cheese and wine
certainly there are things almost worthy
of a pantheon
look at that
girl and imagine
getting to know her
without spoiling the harmony with a real step
look at the haze of nostalgia for
right at this moment
this day
this gray water
a focused fisherman
seems to have caught something
someone has been caught
and someone seems to have caught himself

SEVEN ISLANDS

GRAN CANARIA

lava vomited through the mountain
flowed for a long time to the ocean
directly
it had to cross a village
but weakened it stopped
the black volcanic
crater choked from rage
just the stones stood upright
reddish lumps fused upward together
The blood of the igneous rock earth
scattered in sharply beaten glass
and from the serrated volcanic edge
you can see neighboring islands
chilled by storms and time
you can see an emerging
island seething
among the waves
you can see africa and europe
see the whole world
made smaller by the island
amid the waters

TENERIFE

a small dry land made of two
halves
wet and dry
green and yellow
forests and deserts
pines with unbelievably long
needles
capture the moisture
of fog rain droplets clouds
lakes of translucent water
hiding their roots
under stones
in the hollow depths
and he who finds
an underground looking glass
becomes the watery king
this one old gnarled old man
from a really plain building
the master of the underground water
sells moisture
to the arid south of the island
they say that he bequeathed to his grandchildren
much of the watery elements
at night he stealthily kisses the misty
pines connecting
light and darkness
the earth and sky

LANZAROTE

that's where michel visited
on this luxurious
beach naked lovers used to lay
caressing each other
even during siesta time and at night
and what do you keep busy with here besides
making love on the warm sand
or on such a big bed
you don't amuse yourself every day playing mini-golf
shooting american pool
playing tennis
not infinitely eating
lemon-chicken
in the establishment of smiling chinese
gazpacho and barraquito
among the lazy canary islanders
it's impossible for the spanish god forbid
to demand this
largest lobster
or if you want lobster
in a tiny seaside restaurant
a freaking fifty euros per person
you are left with only making love
in various positions
noting with surprise
the uniformly even tan of two bodies
among the white sheets
and, you still can listen to
the good playing of a guitarist
in a café in a basement with windows
ogle black singers for enjoyment
take pleasure in the live voices and sound
in the taverns simply under the sky
and assume that you're still alive

LA GOMERA

a ferry goes to la gomera
such a clumsy parody
of the titanic
it does not sink it slowly floats
it is also close
idiot tourists
don't listen to the language of the natives' whistling
and try
to find ten differences
in souvenir shops
of this and neighboring islands
they naively steal exotic
lava stones
born in the circular
top of the volcano that
managed to climb from the bottom
of the atlantic
dirty streams flow
during a rain right
into the ocean
spoiling the generally good
appearance of a purely european resort
on an african island
with hotels pools
cheerful retirees
of a united europe
that shine like extinct stars
the fake shine of artificial teeth

LA PALMA

from this mountain
that is called an island
from its very top
from the shaky tooth-stones
it's good to observe
the roundness of the ocean on the horizon
the warm current
and the cold upstream flow
the uncountable shadows of the changing water
at times black backs
of large killer whales
even in warm weather
small clouds are formed
over their lustrous bodies
from their warm breathing and
and uneasy salty droplets
for some reason the nomadic camps of the whales
are not so far away from the shores
perhaps fishing spots attract them
where the ships of fishermen at night
catch the scaled creatures
to the light of lanterns
the fish roam insensately
upward toward the strange bright spots
just like people
until the net halts
their flight
and the killer whale swims in the water and
breathes the air and then
it is harmonious like
an ancient hermaphrodite
looking at the perfection
of the waves and the sky

of the round island amid the ocean
the local climate
and strong drinks
you begin to guess
in what the perfection
of a person should lie
here and
somewhere

EL HIERO

la donna e mobile
of course these two elderly Italian women
sing along
the aria got mixed up
in their thoughts and doesn't come out
freely the way it should
they sing along softly
melodiously
confidently
inconspicuously
politely
a cloud got stuck on
a mountain top
since morning it's been hanging there sedately
bringing moisture to trees and stones
far below in salty waves
fail to quench thirst
they persistently lick
hole-filled lava stones
the italian women are returning from a stroll
to the hotel
they don't notice
small gray lizards
hiding from their footsteps
to the crooked and narrow slits of hiding places
the sun strives
as long as possible to keep the rays
on the surface of the old
oceano atlantico
to change the color of the ancient water
to coat the smooth surface with a scaly luster
why
the aria will end
the cloud will dissipate
the lizards will grow torpid at night
the time for other performers

will come
fat taxi drivers
blasé prostitutes
pompous dealers
fickle ladies
muddle-headed gentlemen
crazed poets
killed guanches[11]
who first and foremost cling to the past
mysteriously erect their pyramids[12]
and mummify the living

---

11 The indigenous inhabitants of the island of Tenerife.

12 For a discussion of the guanches and their pyramids see: https://www.bibliotecapleyades.net/esp_guanches_1.htm.

FUERTEVENTURA

everywhere merry Christmas wishes
feliz navidad
fanciful caves in the depths
of a chunk of dry land
strangely contrast with
the lights of letters on
frames between posts
with the lights of wild oranges
in the green grass
the distant lights of a ship
or island
almost identical things all around
the iron of waves made of stone
of human voices
the rustling of palm leaves
beneath a night wind
slightly different scattered stars
a slightly different spanish articulation
a slightly different paella
but it might just seem like that
it seems we're strolling
it seems we're alive
then why
does conviction increase that
it's time to consider my own
euthanasia
just the influence
of all kinds of amsterdams and mckuens
self-suggestion or
circumspection, foresight
maybe it's better to take care of
a pit six feet deep

with a beautiful view all around
screw the view
but all the same in a human way
suddenly later someone
will address you in a friendly way
as here they say
hola señor escritor[13]

---

13   Hello Mr. Writer in Spanish.

FROM

THE COLLECTION *CONVERSATION*

BEFORE SILENCE

(2005)

I. A GREEN BOAT

***

hauling bodies through landscapes
we constantly remain in
the so called
past
stubbornly appropriating it
falsifying documents and certificates
we persistently write
apocryphal texts
and imaginary stories
instead of learning to capture
and differentiate signs and hints
we train our memory
forcing it
to create a world that did not exist
but it would be worthwhile to get
interested in worlds
colorsounds
and the eternal cloudcathedrals
there
as well as inside yourself

***

I took down my portrait
hid it behind the wardrobe
my essence was too visible in it
one that I didn't feel like looking into
those narrowed eyes and
clenched lips
don't inspire don't let me
smile
let it be for a while in the darkness
maybe the double behind the mirror
or I will change
and maybe the other one will completely disappear
amid the dust

***

to find
the exit from the labyrinth
to wind the thread
having seduced ariadne

one should also kill
or avoid the minotaur
or the dragon here and hereabouts

the happy moment of egress
outward
the rapture from unknown space
that at the same time
may turn out to be
the horror of infinite darkness
to become the boundless night
or simply a quiet night
a kind of kristallnacht

***

but then to separate
consciousness
it will find a way out
through the gratings
will unlock the locks
will pass through unseen secret
passages

it will be able to carry past
the treasure that grew out of
pain and losses
that became your family
treasure
consciousness shouldn't stop
and forget incantations against
time – the cannibal

***

beneath soft velvet wings
of a tender antiday
eyes go blind
from sudden fleeting light

you sense helplessness
return ahead but
then strangely you remember
an exotic white moment
on a faraway and
nearly unreal
terra firma

***

at first foxtail and bluegrass
behind it
clover
sedge
sweet-rush
at last a wobbly bridge
made of willow and
aspen

you try to cross
but make sure not to hurry
far on the other side
beyond a strip of sand
a dark forest that starts right away
monotonous pine needles and grassless
insufferable silence of incense and wax
a sickeningly sweet scent
and then you realize it's not your house there

***

with the key of memory opening
the doors into the past
will I be emboldened to open them all the way
and go
where everyone is still alive
the yellow hills of Kyiv
smell of wild thyme

perhaps there really is no circle
and if there is one why on earth are
nostalgia and recollections
spread out like a silver chain

a bound blind jade
keeps going round and round

***

in the olive-colored water
of the polisiyan[14] river
a tall slim black poplar is reflected
with a serene black kite bird
on its top
the damp canvas of the sky
will not dry
and turns us into
fish in a drag-net
that see just the spot of the sun
somewhere there above

the kite bird is silent
I am silent
the black poplar sighs
a pearl oyster crawls onto the shore
and you can hear its shells
pushing aside the sand
the arrowhead strives
to sway the water with stems
but the water is also silent

a greenish summer runs to the end
the visible part of the day fades
against the violet and deep blue

someone on the road past the meadow
will strike a match

---

14   Polissya is a region that comprises the northern low-lying forested lands of Ukraine.

II. TIME IN RIME

***

she's sleeping close by
and you feel
both completeness and separateness

steady breathing
gives birth to warmth
and illuminates the night
she takes care of your imagination
and rounds space

but when she's away
time takes on the first autumn frost
timid sunset comes
with wind in the dead
branches of trees
with droplets
of the cold sweat of clouds
with a long tiresome road
without any landscapes
without any dreams
without any sense

that's why you think about her

***

to enter into the warm alluring sea
and forget everything
just this moment has value
only this instant is true

the eternal sea
arousing
unfathomable and vast

you are
the nocturnal sea for me

***

when I make love with you
I become a different person
in age
in gender
in temperament in memory

this lasts moments
hours
but the alchemic all-loving
transmutation
happens each time
and proves the reality
of everything experienced with you
and in myself

the tolling of the heart and blood
resonates in my temples
I perceive you
from without and within
I always worry because
every day you are different and new and unfathomable

I begin to remember you and yearn for you again
right at the moment after we part

***

it's really sweet
to kiss you on the lips and seek
your tongue with mine
to kiss your forehead and hair
caress you everywhere
to pretend to be immortal
and actually be so for a bit

life only exists
when I am inside you

but
everything called the future
comes too soon
to be able to ponder it
and prepare a proper response

***

we turn out the light
and dance to the old-time
music
it's not rap or disco
this is the kind of music
you started to appreciate much later in life
it's from another time
and I began to love it the year you were born

we dance
only you
and right now it's better than sex
so simple and nice
then some fast rock and roll
then something nostalgic and slow again

our unhurried dance
will last and last
even
when
you
and
I

***

we're drinking zakarpatsky cognac
you lick your lips
the pink tip of your tongue
night

we'll step outside and real wintry winter
will envelop us
a blind snowstorm

a vortex around a streetlamp
points out the direction of the fall
of snowstars
right at your feet

a pack of homeless dogs
looks and notices
nothing other than
somebody's two dogs
who don't dare approach
the distance of their teeth

FROM

THE COLLECTION *CERTAIN DREAMS,*

OR A KYIV WHICH IS NOT

(2007)

***

They're burning fallen leaves in the garden
and smoke grudgingly flows from the piles.
I'm hastily stealing this day of death,
though it won't be mine.
You need to shorten the lifetime of a rose,
to cover a bush to keep the frost away.
A bird is on guard to a reddish hawthorn—
it bore seeds and died away.
The sky became desired for birds,
and higher for people.
Everywhere the poured-out colors of honey
paint this last world.

***

To draw out some blood—to drink wine.
To break bread—to taste the body.
You are my passion and my guilt;
a sweet sin, cleverly hidden.

It's time to buy six feet of land,
it's time to sign the papers at the notary.
I'd prefer to know: somewhere in the mist,
do the two chimeras disappear—time and space?

The forgiven will go there. You and I.
There everything renewed again appears in a word,
there three worlds merge into a single one,
where there is nothing but love.

***

Those crows that live on Reitarska Street,[15]
nightshades winking with a predatory eye,
stifle their steely rage
and rush above a mute night stream

of alleys, streets and sleepless city squares,
above the slopes of roofs, bell towers and spires;
they fly and caw. Sudden rain
doesn't impede this trinity of black-winged birds.

They fly and their all-piercing movement
covers all of Kyiv, Bald Mountain.[16]
Already locked are thought, vision and hearing;
it seems even the spirit of disobedience is broken.

...Yes, it's just a dream, or a nighttime vision.
Anxious my heart knocks against my ribs.
Not the main road but a side one.
Behind gratings in a courtyard—three black crows.

---

15   A street in the upper central part of the old city in Kyiv that runs between the Golden Gates of Kyiv and St. Sophia Cathedral.

16   Bald Mountain (Lysa hora) is traditionally a place of magic and mystical happenings where witches' covens often meet. Take note of Modest Mussorgsky's musical composition from *Pictures at an Exhibition*, "Night on Bald Mountain."

***

In the dead café
there's cold coffee.
Ristretto and cigarettes—
a daily dish.
Lipstick on the glass.
So it should be.
The waiter studies us
like two amoebas.
Why are we sitting here?
For no reason, of course.
We should get drunk
uncompromisingly.

***

Poured tea, cold coffee.
A shadow fell across a branch
onto a pile of discarded glass
from a table, onto bitter words,
a consumptively beet-colored rug,
and once again onto empty words—
you knew everything—how could you—
onto the past, already rotted.
In the wind the branch moans again
and twitches like an eyebrow,
not broken, but crooked,
it suddenly bent down
and there's no shadows or trace,
but there's only despair, a border—
you're dead and your wife's a stranger
amid the dirty landscape.

***

Gulp, drink up. Don't mention anyone.
Forbid yourself from looking into a black
window. And forget the edge
of twilight. The fog of vodka and tobacco
will envelop you. And this green tea
(the black too though) doesn't cure the pain.
Look left? Here? You knew. Don't take notice either...
Two more double shots—and the song "Young Halya."[17]
And suddenly on the dark floor you
remember her bright face.
And again, you write letters begging forgiveness—
all in your thoughts.
The crust of consciousness...

---

[17] An extremely popular traditional Ukrainian folk song. For a rousing performance of it by the Ukrainian rock band VV on the Maidan see: https://www.youtube.com/watch?v=7bsgXiyaNIo.

FROM

POEMS NOT PUBLISHED IN COLLECTIONS

***

you sleep capriciously
looking at you
I become transformed
just another life

just as before
I cherish the dusky world of insomnia
and the dusky light at night

you breathe and sleep
but I can't get my fill of gazing at you
and fall sleep
and I keep staring intently

in different spaces and conditions
we are closest
and the only thing connecting us is just...

***

sedge
reeds
willow beds
water plants
up to the neck in water
waiting out the flood

the moon at night
looks in horror
at the endless movement
of the flow
of the flow
of the flow

the streams play with the splinters of the moon
sometimes a wet branch
shines silvery

a nighttime flood
and there is no one around

***

an overly intense sense of life
an overly intense half a life
right during an illness when
a languishing
brain
raves over
the future
the past

a piscine mouth snaps at the air
and lungs wait in vain
for it

you dream, remember all
absolutely everything
away with everyone

***

Those colors are gray,
orange,
red,
that flow
from colorful sheets,
from blankets
less important items
from pictures in frames…
Colors that annoy,

until
they go into the night,
the quiet night
with the moon and—not with darkness—
and with dusk
that has purple tenderness above
this city.

Only then
you sleep, you dream,
you see
the calm of knotweed—they
were here once—they
appear during moonlit nights
beneath the already non-existent
sweet cherries and black cherries of the city…
Do you hear? you're sleep…

You live just in dreams
breathe and even
run,
you whisper words to her
that you wouldn't dare say
right to her face—to her
and the moon.
Night; you sleep…
but you know—knotgrass
envelops you.
Dreams.
Kyivan knotgrass still exists—
while you are asleep.

***

the taste of aching in the middle of
the warm gentle night that
clung to the old Mediterranean Sea
from which it came
this is the memory of waves transferred
of everything
that was and will be
or the awareness
of smallness and futility

the leaves of pomegranates and date palms
don't rustle
the terrace above the splinters of the moon in the water
the dark wood of the table in the coffee shop
you drink a flaming B-52
or baileys
listen to the ancient
sgt. pepper's lonely hearts club band
in a tiny little orchestra's version
and gain insight on
how little time you have left
to manage to find
the yet unspoken

The Frontier
28 Contemporary Ukrainian Poets - An Anthology

This anthology reflects a search of the Ukrainian nation for its identity, the roots of which lie deep inside Ukrainian-language poetry. Some of the included poets are well-known locally and internationally; among them are Serhiy Zhadan, Halyna Kruk, Ostap Slyvynsky, Marianna Kijanowska, Oleh Kotsarev, Anna Bagriana and, of course, the living legend of Ukrainian poetry, Vasyl Holoborodko. The next Ukrainian poetic generation also features prominently in the collection. Such poets as Les Beley, Olena Herasymyuk, Myroslav Laiuk, Hanna Malihon, Taras Malkovych, Julia Musakovska, Julia Stahivska and Lyuba Yakimchuk are the ones Ukrainians like to read today, and each of them already has an excellent reputation abroad due to festival appearances and translations to European languages. The work collected here documents poetry in Ukraine responding to challenges of the time by forging a radical new poetic, reconsidering writing techniques and language itself.

Edited and translated from the Ukrainian by Anatoly Kudryavitsky.

A Bilingual Edition.

Buy it > www.glagoslav.com

Acropolis – The Wawel Plays
by Stanisław Wyspiański

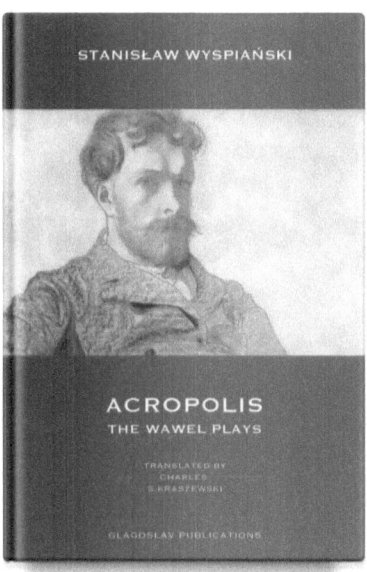

Stanisław Wyspiański (1869-1907) achieved worldwide fame, both as a painter, and Poland's greatest dramatist of the first half of the twentieth century. *Acropolis: the Wawel Plays*, brings together four of Wyspiański's most important dramatic works in a new English translation by Charles S. Kraszewski. All of the plays centre on Wawel Hill: the legendary seat of royal and ecclesiastical power in the poet's native city, the ancient capital of Poland. In these plays, Wyspiański explores the foundational myths of his nation: that of the self-sacrificial Wanda, and the struggle between King Bolesław the Bold and Bishop Stanisław Szczepanowski. In the eponymous play which brings the cycle to an end, Wyspiański carefully considers the value of myth to a nation without political autonomy, soaring in thought into an apocalyptic vision of the future. Richly illustrated with the poet's artwork, *Acropolis: the Wawel Plays* also contains Wyspiański's architectural proposal for the renovation of Wawel Hill, and a detailed critical introduction by the translator. In its plaited presentation of *Bolesław the Bold* and *Skałka*, the translation offers, for the first time, the two plays in the unified, composite format that the poet intended, but was prevented from carrying out by his untimely death.

Buy it > www.glagoslav.com

Pavlo Tychyna:
The Complete Early Poetry Collections

Pavlo Tychyna (1891-1967) is arguably the greatest Ukrainian poet of the twentieth century and has been described as a "tillerman's Orpheus" by Ukrainian poet and literary critic Vasyl Barka. With his innovative poetics, deep spirituality and creative word play, Tychyna deserves a place among the pantheon of his European contemporaries such as T.S. Eliot, Ezra Pound, Rainer Maria Rilke, Federico Garcia Lorca, and Osip Mandelstam. His early collections *Clarinets of the Sun* (1918), *The Plow* (1920), *Instead of Sonnets and Octaves* (1920), The Wind from Ukraine (1924), and his poetic cycle In the Orchestra of the Cosmos (1921) mark the pinnacle of his creativity and poetically document the emotional and spiritual toll of the Revolution of 1917 as well as the Civil War and its aftermath in Ukraine.

Buy it > www.glagoslav.com

The Grand Harmony
by Bohdan Ihor Antonych

The extraordinarily inventive Ukrainian poet and literary critic Bohdan Ihor Antonych (1909-1937), the son of a Catholic priest, died prematurely at the early age of 28 of pneumonia. Originally from the mountainous Lemko region in Poland, where a variant of Ukrainian is spoken, he was home-schooled for the first eleven years of his life because of frequent illness. He began to write poetry in Ukrainian after he moved to the Western Ukrainian city of Lviv to continue his studies at the University of Lviv.

A collection of poems on religious themes written in 1932 and 1933, *The Grand Harmony* is a subtle and supple examination of Antonych's intimately personal journey to faith, with all its revelatory verities as well as self-questioning and doubt. The collection marks the beginning of Antonych's development into one of the greatest poets of his time.

Buy it > www.glagoslav.com

Tsunami
by Anatoly Kurchatkin

Anatoly Kurchatkin's novel, set in Russia and Thailand, ranges in time from the Brezhnev years of political stagnation, when Soviet values seemed set to endure for eternity, through Gorbachev's Perestroika and the following tumultuous and disorientating decades. Under the surface, ancient currents are influencing the destinies of mathematician Rad, art gallery owner Jenny, entrepreneur (and spy?) Dron, American investor Chris, redundant Soviet diplomat Yelena and Thai playboy Tony in a rapidly globalizing world of laptop computers, mobile phones, credit cards and international finance. The fourteenth-century battle in which the Prince of Muscovy, inspired by St Sergius of Radonezh, defeated the Golden Horde of the Mongol Empire foreshadows a modern struggle for the soul of Russia.

Tsunami was shortlisted for the Russian Booker Prize and the Russo-Italian Moscow-Penne Prize.

Buy it > www.glagoslav.com

Dear Reader,

Thank you for purchasing this book.

We at Glagoslav Publications are glad to welcome you, and hope that you find our books to be a source of knowledge and inspiration.

We want to show the beauty and depth of the Slavic region to everyone looking to expand their horizon and learn something new about different cultures, different people, and we believe that with this book we have managed to do just that.

Now that you've got to know us, we want to get to know you. We value communication with our readers and want to hear from you! We offer several options:

– Join our Book Club on Goodreads, Library Thing and Shelfari, and receive special offers and information about our giveaways;

– Share your opinion about our books on Amazon, Barnes & Noble, Waterstones and other bookstores;

– Join us on Facebook and Twitter for updates on our publications and news about our authors;

– Visit our site www.glagoslav.com to check out our Catalogue and subscribe to our Newsletter.

Glagoslav Publications is getting ready to release a new collection and planning some interesting surprises — stay with us to find out!

Glagoslav Publications
Email: contact@glagoslav.com

Glagoslav Publications Catalogue

- *The Time of Women* by Elena Chizhova
- *Andrei Tarkovsky: The Collector of Dreams* by Layla Alexander-Garrett
- *Andrei Tarkovsky - A Life on the Cross* by Lyudmila Boyadzhieva
- *Sin* by Zakhar Prilepin
- *Hardly Ever Otherwise* by Maria Matios
- *Khatyn* by Ales Adamovich
- *The Lost Button* by Irene Rozdobudko
- *Christened with Crosses* by Eduard Kochergin
- *The Vital Needs of the Dead* by Igor Sakhnovsky
- *The Sarabande of Sara's Band* by Larysa Denysenko
- *A Poet and Bin Laden* by Hamid Ismailov
- *Watching The Russians (Dutch Edition)* by Maria Konyukova
- *Kobzar* by Taras Shevchenko
- *The Stone Bridge* by Alexander Terekhov
- *Moryak* by Lee Mandel
- *King Stakh's Wild Hunt* by Uladzimir Karatkevich
- *The Hawks of Peace* by Dmitry Rogozin
- *Harlequin's Costume* by Leonid Yuzefovich
- *Depeche Mode* by Serhii Zhadan
- *The Grand Slam and other stories (Dutch Edition)* by Leonid Andreev
- *METRO 2033 (Dutch Edition)* by Dmitry Glukhovsky
- *METRO 2034 (Dutch Edition)* by Dmitry Glukhovsky
- *A Russian Story* by Eugenia Kononenko
- *Herstories, An Anthology of New Ukrainian Women Prose Writers*
- *The Battle of the Sexes Russian Style* by Nadezhda Ptushkina
- *A Book Without Photographs* by Sergey Shargunov
- *Down Among The Fishes* by Natalka Babina
- *disUNITY* by Anatoly Kudryavitsky
- *Sankya* by Zakhar Prilepin
- *Wolf Messing* by Tatiana Lungin
- *Good Stalin* by Victor Erofeyev

- *Solar Plexus* by Rustam Ibragimbekov
- *Don't Call me a Victim!* by Dina Yafasova
- *Poetin (Dutch Edition)* by Chris Hutchins and Alexander Korobko
- *A History of Belarus* by Lubov Bazan
- *Children's Fashion of the Russian Empire* by Alexander Vasiliev
- *Empire of Corruption - The Russian National Pastime* by Vladimir Soloviev
- *Heroes of the 90s - People and Money. The Modern History of Russian Capitalism*
- *Fifty Highlights from the Russian Literature (Dutch Edition)* by Maarten Tengbergen
- *Bajesvolk (Dutch Edition)* by Mikhail Khodorkovsky
- *Tsarina Alexandra's Diary (Dutch Edition)*
- *Myths about Russia* by Vladimir Medinskiy
- *Boris Yeltsin - The Decade that Shook the World* by Boris Minaev
- *A Man Of Change - A study of the political life of Boris Yeltsin*
- *Sberbank - The Rebirth of Russia's Financial Giant* by Evgeny Karasyuk
- *To Get Ukraine* by Oleksandr Shyshko
- *Asystole* by Oleg Pavlov
- *Gnedich* by Maria Rybakova
- *Marina Tsvetaeva - The Essential Poetry*
- *Multiple Personalities* by Tatyana Shcherbina
- *The Investigator* by Margarita Khemlin
- *The Exile* by Zinaida Tulub
- *Leo Tolstoy – Flight from paradise* by Pavel Basinsky
- *Moscow in the 1930* by Natalia Gromova
- *Laurus (Dutch edition)* by Evgenij Vodolazkin
- *Prisoner* by Anna Nemzer
- *The Crime of Chernobyl - The Nuclear Goulag* by Wladimir Tchertkoff
- *Alpine Ballad* by Vasil Bykau
- *The Complete Correspondence of Hryhory Skovoroda*

- *The Tale of Aypi* by Ak Welsapar
- *Selected Poems* by Lydia Grigorieva
- *The Fantastic Worlds of Yuri Vynnychuk*
- *The Garden of Divine Songs and Collected Poetry of Hryhory Skovoroda*
- *Adventures in the Slavic Kitchen: A Book of Essays with Recipes*
- *Seven Signs of the Lion* by Michael M. Naydan
- *Forefathers' Eve* by Adam Mickiewicz
- *One-Two* by Igor Eliseev
- *Girls, be Good* by Bojan Babić
- *Time of the Octopus* by Anatoly Kucherena
- *Soghomon Tehlirian Memories - The Assassination of Talaat*
- *The Grand Harmony* by Bohdan Ihor Antonych
- *The Selected Lyric Poetry Of Maksym Rylsky*
- *The Shining Light* by Galymkair Mutanov
- *The Frontier: 28 Contemporary Ukrainian Poets - An Anthology*
- *Acropolis - The Wawel Plays* by Stanisław Wyspiański
- *Contours of the City* by Attyla Mohylny
- *Zinnober's Poppets* by Elena Chizhova
- *The Hemingway Game* by Evgeni Grishkovets

More coming soon...

www.ingramcontent.com/pod-product-compliance
Lightning Source LLC
Chambersburg PA
CBHW021127080526
44587CB00012B/1165